PENGUIN BOOKS

Poems of the Great War:
1914–1918

Poems of
the Great War
1914–1918

PENGUIN BOOKS

PENGUIN BOOKS

Published by the Penguin Group
Penguin Books Ltd, 27 Wrights Lane, London w8 5tz, England
Penguin Putnam Inc., 375 Hudson Street, New York, New York 10014, USA
Penguin Books Australia Ltd, Ringwood, Victoria, Australia
Penguin Books Canada Ltd, 10 Alcorn Avenue, Toronto, Ontario, Canada m4v 3b2
Penguin Books (NZ) Ltd, Private Bag 102902, NSMC, Auckland, New Zealand

Penguin Books Ltd, Registered Offices: Harmondsworth, Middlesex, England

This collection first published by Penguin Books 1998
3 5 7 9 10 8 6 4 2

Acknowledgements on p.x constitute an extension of this copyright page

Set in 10/12.5 pt PostScript Monotype Bembo
Typeset by Rowland Phototypesetting Ltd, Bury St Edmunds, Suffolk
Printed in England by Clays Ltd, St Ives plc

Contents

Publisher's Note ix

Acknowledgements x

JOHN MCCRAE In Flanders Fields 1

IVOR GURNEY Strange Hells 2

WILFRED OWEN Anthem for Doomed Youth 3

SIEGFRIED SASSOON How to Die 4

IVOR GURNEY Bach and the Sentry 5

SIEGFRIED SASSOON Died of Wounds 6

FORD MADOX FORD That Exploit of Yours 7

EDMUND BLUNDEN The Watchers 8

EDWARD THOMAS Rain 9

WILFRED OWEN Smile, Smile, Smile 10

ISAAC ROSENBERG August 1914 12

RUPERT BROOKE 1914 13

  I Peace 13

  II Safety 14

  III The Dead 15

  IV The Dead 16

  V The Soldier 17

WILFRED OWEN Mental Cases 18

SIEGFRIED SASSOON The Death-Bed 20

IVOR GURNEY The Silent One 23

ISAAC ROSENBERG Break of Day in the Trenches 24

EDGELL RICKWORD The Soldier Addresses his Body 26

HERBERT READ A Short Poem for Armistice Day 28

WILFRED OWEN Dulce et Decorum est 30

SIEGFRIED SASSOON Trench Duty 32

RICHARD ALDINGTON Trench Idyll 33

EDWARD THOMAS In Memoriam 35

CHARLOTTE MEW The Cenotaph 36

SIEGFRIED SASSOON Stretcher Case 38

EDWARD THOMAS This is No Case of Petty Right
    or Wrong 40

ISAAC ROSENBERG Dead Man's Dump 42

IVOR GURNEY To His Love 47

WILFRED OWEN Insensibility 49

EDMUND BLUNDEN Illusions 52

EDWARD THOMAS Tears 53

WILFRED OWEN The Dead-Beat 54

CHARLES HAMILTON SORLEY 'When you see millions of the
    mouthless dead' 56

SIEGFRIED SASSOON Enemies 57

WILFRED OWEN Greater Love 58

EDMUND BLUNDEN Reunion in War 60

FREDERICK MANNING Grotesque 64

IVOR GURNEY Butchers and Tombs 65

SIEGFRIED SASSOON A Working Party 66

WILFRED OWEN Futility 69

ROBERT GRAVES Recalling War 70

EDMUND BLUNDEN Trench Raid near Hooge 73

WILFRED OWEN Disabled 75

EDWARD THOMAS The Cherry Trees 78

EDMUND BLUNDEN Report on Experience 79

MARGARET POSTGATE COLE The Veteran 80

WILFRED OWEN The Show 81

SIEGFRIED SASSOON The Redeemer 83

IVOR GURNEY Strange Service 85

EDMUND BLUNDEN Third Ypres 87

EDWARD THOMAS The Owl 93

CHARLES HAMILTON SORLEY Two Sonnets 94

SIEGFRIED SASSOON Banishment 96

WILFRED OWEN Arms and the Boy 97

EDMUND BLUNDEN Preparations for Victory 98

IVOR GURNEY Pain 100

SIEGFRIED SASSOON Repression of War Experience 101

WILFRED OWEN The Send-off 103

SIEGFRIED SASSOON Glory of Women 105

THOMAS HARDY Channel Firing 106

WILFRED OWEN The Sentry 108

IVOR GURNEY De Profundis 110

SIEGFRIED SASSOON Suicide in the Trenches 112

WILFRED OWEN Strange Meeting 113

F. S. FLINT Lament 115

WILFRED OWEN Exposure 117

SIEGFRIED SASSOON Counter-Attack 120

IVOR GURNEY Photographs 122

WILFRED OWEN Spring Offensive 124

ALICE MEYNELL Summer in England, 1914 127

SIEGFRIED SASSOON Lamentations 129

WILFRED OWEN Conscious 130

IVOR GURNEY To the Prussians of England 131

SIEGFRIED SASSOON The Hero 132

EDMUND BLUNDEN The Welcome 133

WILFRED OWEN Apologia pro Poemate Meo 135

SIEGFRIED SASSOON Attack 137

WILFRED OWEN Wild with all Regrets 138

RICHARD ALDINGTON In the Trenches 140

WILFRED OWEN The End 142

SIEGFRIED SASSOON Does it Matter? 143

MAY WEDDERBURN CANNAN Lamplight 144

Publisher's Note

This selection of poetry is intended to be an introduction to the great wealth of First World War poetry, and makes no attempt to be comprehesive. The sequence is random and drawn from several sources, mixing both well-known and less familiar poetry, and is limited to poems written in English. The collection is published to commemorate the eightieth anniversary of Armistice.

Acknowledgements

We are indebted to the copyright holders for permission to reprint certain poems:

RICHARD ALDINGTON: for 'In the Trenches' and 'Trench Idyll' from *The Complete Poems* (Allan Wingate, 1948), © Estate of Richard Aldington, to Rosica Colin Ltd; EDMUND BLUNDEN: for 'Third Ypres' from *Undertones of War* (Penguin, 1937), and 'Preparations for Victory', 'Illusions', 'Trench Raid near Hooge', 'The Welcome', 'Reunion in War', and 'The Watchers' from POEMS 1914–1930 (Cobden-Sanderson, 1930), to The Peters, Fraser & Dunlop Group Ltd on behalf of the Estate of Edmund Blunden; MAY WEDDERBURN CANNAN: for 'Lamplight' from *In Wartime* (Blackwell, 1917), to James C. Slater; MARGARET POSTGATE COLE: for 'The Veteran' from *Poems* (Allen & Unwin, 1918), to David Higham Associates Ltd; F. S. FLINT: 'Lament' from *Otherworld/Cadences* (Poetry Bookshop, 1920); FORD MADOX FORD: for 'That Exploit of Yours' from *On Heaven/ and Other Poems* (Poetry Bookshop, 1918), to David Higham Associates Ltd; ROBERT GRAVES: for 'Recalling War' from *Collected Poems* (Cassell, 1975), to Carcanet Press Ltd; IVOR

Sassoon, to George Sassoon and the Barbara Levy Literary Agency.

In spite of all possible efforts, we have been unable to trace the Estate of F. S. Flint at the time of going to press. The publishers apologize for including his poem without acknowledgement, and would be pleased to hear from the copyright holder, in order to rectify this omission at the earliest opportunity.

JOHN McCRAE
In Flanders Fields

In Flanders fields the poppies blow
Between the crosses, row on row,
   That mark our place; and in the sky
   The larks, still bravely singing, fly
Scarce heard amid the guns below.

We are the Dead. Short days ago
We lived, felt dawn, saw sunset glow,
   Loved and were loved, and now we lie
         In Flanders fields.

Take up our quarrel with the foe:
To you from failing hands we throw
   The torch; be yours to hold it high.
   If ye break faith with us who die
We shall not sleep, though poppies grow
         In Flanders fields.

Strange Hells

There are strange hells within the minds war made
Not so often, not so humiliatingly afraid
As one would have expected – the racket and fear guns
    made.
One hell the Gloucester soldiers they quite put out:
Their first bombardment, when in combined black shout
Of fury, guns aligned, they ducked lower their heads
And sang with diaphragms fixed beyond all dreads,
That tin and stretched-wire tinkle, that blither of tune:
'Après la guerre fini', till hell all had come down,
Twelve-inch, six-inch, and eighteen pounders hammering
    hell's thunders.

Where are they now, on state-doles, or showing shop-
    patterns
Or walking town to town sore in borrowed tatterns
Or begged. Some civic routine one never learns.
The heart burns – but has to keep out of face how heart
    burns.

WILFRED OWEN
Anthem for Doomed Youth

What passing-bells for these who die as cattle?
    Only the monstrous anger of the guns.
    Only the stuttering rifles' rapid rattle
Can patter out their hasty orisons.
No mockeries for them: no prayers nor bells,
Nor any voice of mourning save the choirs, –
The shrill, demented choirs of wailing shells;
And bugles calling for them from sad shires.

What candles may be held to speed them all?
    Not in the hands of boys, but in their eyes
Shall shine the holy glimmers of goodbyes.
    The pallor of girls' brows shall be their pall;
Their flowers the tenderness of patient minds,
And each slow dusk a drawing-down of blinds.

How to Die

Dark clouds are smouldering into red
   While down the craters morning burns.
The dying soldier shifts his head
   To watch the glory that returns;
He lifts his fingers toward the skies
   Where holy brightness breaks in flame;
Radiance reflected in his eyes,
   And on his lips a whispered name.

You'd think, to hear some people talk,
   That lads go West with sobs and curses,
And sullen faces white as chalk,
   Hankering for wreaths and tombs and hearses.
But they've been taught the way to do it
   Like Christian soldiers; not with haste
And shuddering groans; but passing through it
   With due regard for decent taste.

Bach and the Sentry

Watching the dark my spirit rose in flood
  On that most dearest Prelude of my delight.
The low-lying mist lifted its hood,
  The October stars showed nobly in clear night.

When I return, and to real music-making,
  And play that Prelude, how will it happen then?
Shall I feel as I felt, a sentry hardly waking,
  With a dull sense of No Man's Land again?

Died of Wounds

His wet white face and miserable eyes
Brought nurses to him more than groans and sighs:
But hoarse and low and rapid rose and fell
His troubled voice: he did the business well.

The ward grew dark; but he was still complaining
And calling out for 'Dickie'. 'Curse the Wood!
'It's time to go. O Christ, and what's the good?
'We'll never take it, and it's always raining.'

I wondered where he'd been; then heard him shout,
'They snipe like hell! O Dickie, don't go out' . . .
I fell asleep . . . Next morning he was dead;
And some Slight Wound lay smiling on the bed.

That Exploit of Yours

I meet two soldiers sometimes here in Hell
The one, with a tear in the seat of his red pantaloons
Was stuck by a pitchfork,
Climbing a wall to steal apples.

The second has a seeming silver helmet,
Having died from the fall of his horse on some
    tram-lines
In Dortmund.

These two
˙Meeting in the vaulted and vaporous caverns of Hell
Exclaim always in identical tones:
'I at least have done my duty to Society and the
    Fatherland!'
It is strange how the cliché prevails . . .
For I will bet my hat that you who sent me here to
    Hell
Are saying the selfsame words at this very moment
Concerning that exploit of yours.

EDMUND BLUNDEN
The Watchers

I heard the challenge 'Who goes there?'
Close-kept but mine through midnight air;
I answered and was recognized
And passed, and kindly thus advised:
'There's someone crawlin' through the grass
By the red ruin, or there was,
And them machine guns been a firin'
All the time the chaps was wirin',
So sir if you're goin' out
You'll keep your 'ead well down no doubt.'

When will the stern fine 'Who goes there?'
Meet me again in midnight air?
And the gruff sentry's kindness, when
Will kindness have such power again?
It seems as, now I wake and brood,
And know my hour's decrepitude,
That on some dewy parapet
The sentry's spirit gazes yet,
Who will not speak with altered tone
When I at last am seen and known.

EDWARD THOMAS
Rain

Rain, midnight rain, nothing but the wild rain
On this bleak hut, and solitude, and me
Remembering again that I shall die
And neither hear the rain nor give it thanks
For washing me cleaner than I have been
Since I was born into this solitude.
Blessed are the dead that the rain rains upon:
But here I pray that none whom once I loved
Is dying to-night or lying still awake
Solitary, listening to the rain,
Either in pain or thus in sympathy
Helpless among the living and the dead,
Like a cold water among broken reeds,
Myriads of broken reeds all still and stiff,
Like me who have no love which this wild rain
Has not dissolved except the love of death,
If love it be for what is perfect and
Cannot, the tempest tells me, disappoint.

Smile, Smile, Smile

Head to limp head, the sunk-eyed wounded scanned
Yesterday's Mail: the casualties (typed small)
And (large) Vast Booty from our Latest Haul.
Also, they read of Cheap Homes, not yet planned;
For, said the paper, When this war is done
The men's first instinct will be making homes.
Meanwhile their foremost need is aerodromes,
It being certain war has just begun.
Peace would do wrong to our undying dead, –
The sons we offered might regret they died
If we got nothing lasting in their stead.
We must be solidly indemnified.
Though all be worthy Victory which all bought,
We rulers sitting in this ancient spot
Would wrong our very selves if we forgot
The greatest glory will be theirs who fought,
Who kept this nation in integrity.
Nation? – The half-limbed readers did not chafe
But smiled at one another curiously
Like secret men who know their secret safe.
This is the thing they know and never speak,

That England one by one had fled to France
(Not many elsewhere now save under France).
Pictures of these broad smiles appear each week,
And people in whose voice real feeling rings
Say: How they smile! They're happy now, poor things.

August 1914

What in our lives is burnt
In the fire of this?
The heart's dear granary?
The much we shall miss?

Three lives hath one life –
Iron, honey, gold.
The gold, the honey gone –
Left is the hard and cold.

Iron are our lives
Molten right through our youth.
A burnt space through ripe fields
A fair mouth's broken tooth.

1914

I Peace

Now, God be thanked Who has matched us with His
    hour,
   And caught our youth, and wakened us from sleeping,
With hand made sure, clear eye, and sharpened power,
   To turn, as swimmers into cleanness leaping,
Glad from a world grown old and cold and weary,
   Leave the sick hearts that honour could not move,
And half-men, and their dirty songs and dreary,
   And all the little emptiness of love!

Oh! we, who have known shame, we have found release
    there,
   Where there's no ill, no grief, but sleep has mending,
     Naught broken save this body, lost but breath;
Nothing to shake the laughing heart's long peace there
   But only agony, and that has ending;
     And the worst friend and enemy is but Death.

II Safety

Dear! of all happy in the hour, most blest
    He who has found our hid security,
Assured in the dark tides of the world at rest,
    And heard our word, 'Who is so safe as we?'
We have found safety with all things undying,
    The winds, and morning, tears of men and mirth,
The deep night, and birds singing, and clouds flying,
    And sleep, and freedom, and the autumnal earth.
We have built a house that is not for Time's throwing.
    We have gained a peace unshaken by pain for ever.
War knows no power. Safe shall be my going,
    Secretly armed against all death's endeavour;
Safe though all safety's lost; safe where men fall;
And if these poor limbs die, safest of all.

III The Dead

Blow out, you bugles, over the rich Dead!
    There's none of these so lonely and poor of old,
    But, dying, has made us rarer gifts than gold.
These laid the world away; poured out the red
Sweet wine of youth; gave up the years to be
    Of work and joy, and that unhoped serene,
    That men call age; and those who would have been,
Their sons, they gave, their immortality.

Blow, bugles, blow! They brought us, for our dearth,
    Holiness, lacked so long, and Love, and Pain.
Honour has come back, as a king, to earth,
    And paid his subjects with a royal wage;
And Nobleness walks in our ways again;
    And we have come into our heritage.

IV The Dead

These hearts were woven of human joys and cares,
　　Washed marvellously with sorrow, swift to mirth,
The years had given them kindness. Dawn was theirs,
　　And sunset, and the colours of the earth.
These had seen movement, and heard music; known
　　Slumber and waking; loved; gone proudly friended;
Felt the quick stir of wonder; sat alone;
　　Touched flowers and furs and cheeks. All this is ended.

There are waters blown by changing winds to laughter
And lit by the rich skies, all day. And after,
　　Frost, with a gesture, stays the waves that dance
And wandering loveliness. He leaves a white
　　Unbroken glory, a gathered radiance,
A width, a shining peace, under the night.

V The Soldier

If I should die, think only this of me:
    That there's some corner of a foreign field
That is for ever England. There shall be
    In that rich earth a richer dust concealed;
A dust whom England bore, shaped, made aware,
    Gave, once, her flowers to love, her ways to roam,
A body of England's, breathing English air,
    Washed by the rivers, blest by suns of home.

And think, this heart, all evil shed away,
    A pulse in the eternal mind, no less
        Gives somewhere back the thoughts by England
            given;
Her sights and sounds; dreams happy as her day;
    And laughter, learnt of friends; and gentleness,
        In hearts at peace, under an English heaven.

Mental Cases

Who are these? Why sit they here in twilight?
Wherefore rock they, purgatorial shadows,
Drooping tongues from jaws that slob their relish,
Baring teeth that leer like skulls' tongues wicked?
Stroke on stroke of pain, – but what slow panic,
Gouged these chasms round their fretted sockets?
Ever from their hair and through their hand palms
Misery swelters. Surely we have perished
Sleeping, and walk hell; but who these hellish?

– These are men whose minds the Dead have
    ravished.
Memory fingers in their hair of murders,
Multitudinous murders they once witnessed.
Wading sloughs of flesh these helpless wander,
Treading blood from lungs that had loved laughter.
Always they must see these things and hear them,
Batter of guns and shatter of flying muscles,
Carnage incomparable and human squander
Rucked too thick for these men's extrication.

Therefore still their eyeballs shrink tormented
Back into their brains, because on their sense
Sunlight seems a bloodsmear: night comes
    blood-black;
Dawn breaks open like a wound that bleeds afresh
– Thus their heads wear this hilarious, hideous,
Awful falseness of set-smiling corpses.
– Thus their hands are plucking at each other;
Picking at the rope-knouts of their scourging;
Snatching after us who smote them, brother,
Pawing us who dealt them war and madness.

SIEGFRIED SASSOON
The Death-Bed

He drowsed and was aware of silence heaped
Round him, unshaken as the steadfast walls;
Aqueous like floating rays of amber light,
Soaring and quivering in the wings of sleep.
Silence and safety; and his mortal shore
Lipped by the inward, moonless waves of death.

Someone was holding water to his mouth.
He swallowed, unresisting; moaned and dropped
Through crimson gloom to darkness; and forgot
The opiate throb and ache that was his wound.
    Water – calm, sliding green above the weir.
    Water – a sky-lit alley for his boat,
    Bird-voiced, and bordered with reflected flowers
    And shaken hues of summer; drifting down,
    He dipped contented oars, and sighed, and slept.

Night, with a gust of wind, was in the ward,
Blowing the curtain to a glimmering curve.
Night. He was blind; he could not see the stars

Glinting among the wraiths of wandering cloud;
Queer blots of colour, purple, scarlet, green,
Flickered and faded in his drowning eyes.

Rain – he could hear it rustling through the dark;
Fragrance and passionless music woven as one;
Warm rain on drooping roses; pattering showers
That soak the woods; not the harsh rain that sweeps
Behind the thunder, but a trickling peace,
Gently and slowly washing life away.

He stirred, shifting his body; then the pain
Leapt like a prowling beast, and gripped and tore
His groping dreams with grinding claws and fangs.
   But someone was beside him; soon he lay
   Shuddering because that evil thing had passed.
   And death, who'd stepped toward him, paused and
      stared.

Light many lamps and gather round his bed.
Lend him your eyes, warm blood, and will to live.
Speak to him; rouse him; you may save him yet.
He's young; he hated War; how should he die
When cruel old campaigners win safe through?

But death replied: 'I choose him.' So he went,
And there was silence in the summer night;
Silence and safety; and the veils of sleep.
Then, far away, the thudding of the guns.

IVOR GURNEY
The Silent One

Who died on the wires, and hung there, one of two –
Who for his hours of life had chattered through
Infinite lovely chatter of Bucks accent:
Yet faced unbroken wires; stepped over, and went
A noble fool, faithful to his stripes – and ended.
But I weak, hungry, and willing only for the chance
Of line – to fight in the line, lay down under unbroken
Wires, and saw the flashes and kept unshaken,
Till the politest voice – a finicking accent, said:
'Do you think you might crawl through there: there's
    a hole'
Darkness, shot at: I smiled, as politely replied –
'I'm afraid not, Sir.' There was no hole no way to be
    seen
Nothing but chance of death, after tearing of clothes.
Kept flat, and watched the darkness, hearing bullets
    whizzing –
And thought of music – and swore deep heart's deep
    oaths
(Polite to God) and retreated and came on again,
Again retreated – and a second time faced the screen

ISAAC ROSENBERG
Break of Day in the Trenches

The darkness crumbles away –
It is the same old druid Time as ever.
Only a live thing leaps my hand –
A queer sardonic rat –
As I pull the parapet's poppy
To stick behind my ear.
Droll rat, they would shoot you if they knew
Your cosmopolitan sympathies.
Now you have touched this English hand
You will do the same to a German –
Soon, no doubt, if it be your pleasure
To cross the sleeping green between.
It seems you inwardly grin as you pass
Strong eyes, fine limbs, haughty athletes
Less chanced than you for life,
Bonds to the whims of murder,
Sprawled in the bowels of the earth,
The torn fields of France.
What do you see in our eyes
At the shrieking iron and flame
Hurled through still heavens?

What quaver – what heart aghast?
Poppies whose roots are in man's veins
Drop, and are ever dropping;
But mine in my ear is safe,
Just a little white with the dust.

The Soldier Addresses his Body

I shall be mad if you get smashed about,
we've had good times together, you and I;
although you groused a bit when luck was out,
say a girl turned us down, or we went dry.

But there's a world of things we haven't done,
countries not seen, where people do strange things;
eat fish alive, and mimic in the sun
the solemn gestures of their stone-grey kings.

I've heard of forests that are dim at noon
where snakes and creepers wrestle all day long;
where vivid beasts grow pale with the full moon,
gibber and cry, and wail a mad old song;

because at the full moon the Hippogriff
with crinkled ivory snout and agate feet,
with his green eye will glare them cold and stiff
for the coward Wyvern to come down and eat.

Vodka and kvass, and bitter mountain wines
we've never drunk; nor snatched the bursting grapes
to pelt slim girls among Sicilian vines,
who'd flicker through the leaves, faint frolic shapes.

Yes, there's a world of things we've never done,
but it's a sweat to knock them into rhyme,
let's have a drink, and give the cards a run
and leave dull verse to the dull peaceful time.

A Short Poem for Armistice Day

Gather or take fierce degree
trim the lamp set out for sea
here we are at the workmen's entrance
clock in and shed your eminence.

Notwithstanding, work it diverse ways
work it diverse days, multiplying four digestions
here we make artificial flowers
of paper tin and metal thread.

One eye one leg one arm one lung
a syncopated sick heart-beat
the record is not nearly worn
that weaves a background to our work.

I have no power therefore have patience
these flowers have no sweet scent
no lustre in the petal no increase
from fertilizing flies and bees.

No seed they have no seed
their tendrils are of wire and grip
the buttonhole the lip
and never fade

And will not fade though life
and lustre go in genuine flowers
and men like flowers are cut
and wither on a stem

And will not fade a year or more
I stuck one in a candlestick
and there it clings about the socket
I have no power therefore have patience.

Dulce et Decorum est

Bent double, like old beggars under sacks,
Knock-kneed, coughing like hags, we cursed through
    sludge,
Till on the haunting flares we turned our backs,
And towards our distant rest began to trudge.
Men marched asleep. Many had lost their boots,
But limped on, blood-shod. All went lame, all blind;
Drunk with fatigue; deaf even to the hoots
Of gas-shells dropping softly behind.

Gas! GAS! Quick, boys! – An ecstasy of fumbling
Fitting the clumsy helmets just in time,
But someone still was yelling out and stumbling
And flound'ring like a man in fire or lime. –
Dim through the misty panes and thick green light,
As under a green sea, I saw him drowning.

In all my dreams before my helpless sight
He plunges at me, guttering, choking, drowning.

If in some smothering dreams, you too could pace
Behind the wagon that we flung him in,
And watch the white eyes writhing in his face,
His hanging face, like a devil's sick of sin,
If you could hear, at every jolt, the blood
Come gargling from the froth-corrupted lungs
Bitten as the cud
Of vile, incurable sores on innocent tongues, –
My friend, you would not tell with such high zest
To children ardent for some desperate glory,
The old Lie: *Dulce et decorum est*
Pro patria mori.

Trench Duty

Shaken from sleep, and numbed and scarce awake,
Out in the trench with three hours' watch to take,
I blunder through the splashing mirk; and then
Hear the gruff muttering voices of the men
Crouching in cabins candle-chinked with light.
Hark! There's the big bombardment on our right
Rumbling and bumping; and the dark's a glare
Of flickering horror in the sectors where
We raid the Boche; men waiting, stiff and chilled,
Or crawling on their bellies through the wire.
'What? Stretcher-bearers wanted? Some one killed?'
Five minutes ago I heard a sniper fire:
Why did he do it? . . . Starlight overhead –
Blank stars. I'm wide-awake; and some chap's dead.

RICHARD ALDINGTON
Trench Idyll

We sat together in the trench,
He on a lump of frozen earth
Blown in the night before,
I on an unexploded shell;
And smoked and talked, like exiles,
Of how pleasant London was,
Its women, restaurants, night clubs, theatres,
How at that very hour
The taxi-cabs were taking folk to dine . . .
Then we sat silent for a while
As a machine-gun swept the parapet.

He said:
'I've been here on and off two years
And seen only one man killed'.

'That's odd.'

'The bullet hit him in the throat;
He fell in a heap on the fire-step,
And called out 'My God! *dead!*'

'Good Lord, how terrible!'

'Well, as to that, the nastiest job I've had
Was last year on this very front
Taking the discs at night from men
Who'd hung for six months on the wire
Just over there.
The worst of all was
They fell to pieces at a touch.
Thank God we couldn't see their faces;
They had gas helmets on . . .'

I shivered;
'It's rather cold here, sir, suppose we move?'

EDWARD THOMAS
In Memoriam

The flowers left thick at nightfall in the wood
This Eastertide call into mind the men,
Now far from home, who, with their sweethearts,
    should
Have gathered them and will do never again.

The Cenotaph

Not yet will those measureless fields be green again
Where only yesterday the wild sweet blood of wonderful
    youth was shed;
There is a grave whose earth must hold too long, too deep
    a stain,
Though for ever over it we may speak as proudly as we may
    tread.
But here, where the watchers by lonely hearths from the
    thrust of an inward sword have more slowly bled,
We shall build the Cenotaph: Victory, winged, with Peace
    winged too, at the column's head.
And over the stairway, at the foot – oh! here, leave desolate,
    passionate hands to spread
Violets, roses, and laurel, with the small, sweet, twinkling
    country things.
Speaking so wistfully of other Springs,
From the little gardens of little places where son or sweetheart
    was born and bred.
In splendid sleep, with a thousand brothers
        To lovers – to mothers
        Here, too, lies he:

Under the purple, the green, the red,
It is all young life: it must break some women's hearts to
    see
Such a brave, gay coverlet to such a bed!
Only, when all is done and said,
God is not mocked and neither are the dead.
For this will stand in our Market-place –
        Who'll sell, who'll buy
        (Will you or I
Lie each to each with better grace)?
While looking into every busy whore's and huckster's
    face
As they drive their bargains, is the Face
Of God: and some young, piteous, murdered face.

Stretcher Case

He woke; the clank and racket of the train
Kept time with angry throbbings in his brain.
Then for a while he lapsed and drowsed again.
At last he lifted his bewildered eyes
And blinked, and rolled them sidelong; hills and
    skies,
Heavily wooded, hot with August haze,
And, slipping backward, golden for his gaze,
Acres of harvest.

          Feebly now he drags
Exhausted ego back from glooms and quags
And blasting tumult, terror, hurtling glare,
To calm and brightness, havens of sweet air.
He sighed, confused; then drew a cautious breath;
This level journeying was no ride through death.
'If I were dead,' he mused, 'there'd be no thinking –
Only some plunging underworld of sinking,
And hueless, shifting welter where I'd drown.'

Then he remembered that his name was Brown.

But was he back in Blighty? Slow he turned,
Till in his heart thanksgiving leapt and burned.
There shone the blue serene, the prosperous land,
Trees, cows and hedges; skipping these, he scanned
Large, friendly names, that change not with the year,
Lung Tonic, Mustard, Liver Pills and Beer.

This is No Case of Petty Right or Wrong

This is no case of petty right or wrong
That politicians or philosophers
Can judge. I hate not Germans, nor grow hot
With love of Englishmen, to please newspapers.
Beside my hate for one fat patriot
My hatred of the Kaiser is love true: –
A kind of god he is, banging a gong.
But I have not to choose between the two,
Or between justice and injustice. Dinned
With war and argument I read no more
Than in the storm smoking along the wind
Athwart the wood. Two witches' cauldrons roar.
From one the weather shall rise clear and gay;
Out of the other an England beautiful
And like her mother that died yesterday.
Little I know or care if, being dull,
I shall miss something that historians
Can rake out of the ashes when perchance
The phoenix broods serene above their ken.
But with the best and meanest Englishmen

I am one in crying, God save England, lest
We lose what never slaves and cattle blessed.
The ages made her that made us from dust:
She is all we know and live by, and we trust
She is good and must endure, loving her so:
And as we love ourselves we hate her foe.

ISAAC ROSENBERG
Dead Man's Dump

The plunging limbers over the shattered track
Racketed with their rusty freight,
Stuck out like many crowns of thorns,
And the rusty stakes like sceptres old
To stay the flood of brutish men
Upon our brothers dear.

The wheels lurched over sprawled dead
But pained them not, though their bones
    crunched,
Their shut mouths made no moan.
They lie there huddled, friend and forman,
Man born of man, and born of woman,
And shells go crying over them
From night till night and now.

Earth has waited for them,
All the time of their growth
Fretting for their decay:

Now she has them at last!
In the strength of their strength
Suspended – stopped and held.

What fierce imaginings their dark souls lit?
Earth! have they gone into you!
Somewhere they must have gone,
And flung on your hard back
Is their soul's sack
Emptied of God-ancestralled essences.
Who hurled them out? Who hurled?

None saw their spirits' shadow shake the grass,
Or stood aside for the half used life to pass
Out of those doomed nostrils and the doomed
    mouth,
When the swift iron burning bee
Drained the wild honey of their youth.

What of us who, flung on the shrieking pyre,
Walk, our usual thoughts untouched,
Our lucky limbs as on ichor fed,
Immortal seeming ever?

Perhaps when the flames beat loud on us,
A fear may choke in our veins
And the startled blood may stop.

The air is loud with death,
The dark air spurts with fire,
The explosions ceaseless are.
Timelessly now, some minutes past,
These dead strode time with vigorous life,
Till the shrapnel called 'An end!'
But not to all. In bleeding pangs
Some borne on stretchers dreamed of home,
Dear things, war-blotted from their hearts.

Maniac Earth! howling and flying, your bowel
Seared by the jagged fire, the iron love,
The impetuous storm of savage love.
Dark Earth! dark Heavens! swinging in chemic
    smoke,
What dead are born when you kiss each soundless
    soul
With lightning and thunder from your mined heart,
Which man's self dug, and his blind fingers loosed?

44

A man's brains splattered on
A stretcher-bearer's face;
His shook shoulders slipped their load,
But when they bent to look again
The drowning soul was sunk too deep
For human tenderness.
They left this dead with the older dead,
Stretched at the cross roads.

Burnt black by strange decay
Their sinister faces lie,
The lid over each eye,
The grass and coloured clay
More motion have than they,
Joined to the great sunk silences.

Here is one not long dead;
His dark hearing caught our far wheels,
And the choked soul stretched weak hands
To reach the living word the far wheels said,
The blood-dazed intelligence beating for light,
Crying through the suspense of the far torturing
    wheels

Swift for the end to break
Or the wheels to break,
Cried as the tide of the world broke over his
    sight.

Will they come? Will they ever come?
Even as the mixed hoofs of the mules,
The quivering-bellied mules,
And the rushing wheels all mixed
With his tortured upturned sight.
So we crashed round the bend,
We heard his weak scream,
We heard his very last sound,
And our wheels grazed his dead face.

IVOR GURNEY
To His Love

He's gone, and all our plans
   Are useless indeed.
We'll walk no more on Cotswold
   Where the sheep feed
   Quietly and take no heed.

His body that was so quick
   Is not as you
Knew it, on Severn river
   Under the blue
   Driving our small boat through.

You would not know him now . . .
   But still he died
Nobly, so cover him over
   With violets of pride
   Purple from Severn side.

Cover him, cover him soon!
  And with thick-set
Masses of memoried flowers —
  Hide that red wet
  Thing I must somehow forget.

WILFRED OWEN
Insensibility

I

Happy are men who yet before they are killed
Can let their veins run cold.
Whom no compassion fleers
Or makes their feet
Sore on the alleys cobbled with their brothers.
The front line withers,
But they are troops who fade, not flowers
For poets' tearful fooling:
Men, gaps for filling
Losses who might have fought
Longer; but no one bothers.

II

And some cease feeling
Even themselves or for themselves.
Dullness best solves
The tease and doubt of shelling,
And Chance's strange arithmetic
Comes simpler than the reckoning of their shilling.
They keep no check on Armies' decimation.

III

Happy are these who lose imagination:
They have enough to carry with ammunition.
Their spirit drags no pack.
Their old wounds save with cold can not more
 ache.
Having seen all things red,
Their eyes are rid
Of the hurt of the colour of blood for ever.
And terror's first constriction over,
Their hearts remain small drawn.
Their senses in some scorching cautery of battle
Now long since ironed,
Can laugh among the dying, unconcerned.

IV

Happy the soldier home, with not a notion
How somewhere, every dawn, some men attack,
And many sighs are drained.
Happy the lad whose mind was never trained:
His days are worth forgetting more than not.
He sings along the march
Which we march taciturn, because of dusk,
The long, forlorn, relentless trend
From larger day to huger night.

V

We wise, who with a thought besmirch
Blood over all our soul,
How should we see our task
But through his blunt and lashless eyes?
Alive, he is not vital overmuch;
Dying, not mortal overmuch;
Nor sad, nor proud,
Nor curious at all.
He cannot tell
Old men's placidity from his.

VI

But cursed are dullards whom no cannon stuns,
That they should be as stones.
Wretched are they, and mean
With paucity that never was simplicity.
By choice they made themselves immune
To pity and whatever mourns in man
Before the last sea and the hapless stars;
Whatever mourns when many leave these shores;
Whatever shares
The eternal reciprocity of tears.

Illusions

Trenches in the moonlight, in the lulling moonlight
Have had their loveliness; when dancing dewy grasses
Caressed us passing along their earthy lanes;
When the crucifix hanging over was strangely illumined,
And one imagined music, one even heard the brave bird
In the sighing orchards flute above the weedy well.
There are such moments; forgive me that I note them,
Nor gloze that there comes soon the nemesis of beauty,
In the fluttering relics that at first glimmer wakened
Terror – the no-man's ditch suddenly forking:
There, the enemy's best with bombs and brains and courage!
– Softly, swiftly, at once be animal and angel –
But O no, no, they're Death's malkins dangling in the wire
    For the moon's interpretation.

EDWARD THOMAS
Tears

It seems I have no tears left. They should have
    fallen –
Their ghosts, if tears have ghosts, did fall – that day
When twenty hounds streamed by me, not yet
    combed out
But still all equals in their rage of gladness
Upon the scent, made one, like a great dragon
In Blooming Meadow that bends towards the sun
And once bore hops: and on that other day
When I stepped out from the double-shadowed
    Tower
Into an April morning, stirring and sweet
And warm. Strange solitude was there and silence.
A mightier charm than any in the Tower
Possessed the courtyard. They were changing guard,
Soldiers in line, young English countrymen,
Fair-haired and ruddy, in white tunics. Drums
And fifes were playing 'The British Grenadiers'.
The men, the music piercing that solitude
And silence, told me truths I had not dreamed,
And have forgotten since their beauty passed.

WILFRED OWEN
The Dead-Beat

He dropped, – more sullenly than wearily,
Lay stupid like a cod, heavy like meat,
And none of us could kick him to his feet;
Just blinked at my revolver, blearily;
– Didn't appear to know a war was on,
Or see the blasted trench at which he stared.
'I'll do 'em in,' he whined. 'If this hand's spared,
I'll murder them, I will.'

              A low voice said,
'It's Blighty, p'raps, he sees; his pluck's all gone,
Dreaming of all the valiant, that *aren't* dead:
Bold uncles, smiling ministerially;
Maybe his brave young wife, getting her fun
In some new home, improved materially.
It's not these stiffs have crazed him; nor the Hun.'

We sent him down at last, out of the way.
Unwounded; – stout lad, too, before that strafe.
Malingering? Stretcher-bearers winked, 'Not half!'

Next day I heard the Doc's well-whiskied laugh:
'That scum you sent last night soon died. Hooray!'

CHARLES HAMILTON SORLEY

'When you see millions of the mouthless dead'

When you see millions of the mouthless dead
Across your dreams in pale battalions go,
Say not soft things as other men have said,
That you'll remember. For you need not so.
Give them not praise. For, deaf, how should they
    know
It is not curses heaped on each gashed head?
Nor tears. Their blind eyes see not your tears flow.
Nor honour. It is easy to be dead.
Say only this, 'They are dead.' Then add thereto,
'Yet many a better one has died before.'
Then, scanning all the o'ercrowded mass, should
    you
Perceive one face that you loved heretofore,
It is a spook. None wears the face you knew.
Great death has made all his for evermore.

SIEGFRIED SASSOON
Enemies

He stood alone in some queer sunless place
Where Armageddon ends. Perhaps he longed
For days he might have lived; but his young face
Gazed forth untroubled: and suddenly there
    thronged
Round him the hulking Germans that I shot
When for his death my brooding rage was hot.

He stared at them, half-wondering; and then
They told him how I'd killed them for his sake –
Those patient, stupid, sullen ghosts of men;
And still there seemed no answer he could make.
At last he turned and smiled. One took his hand
Because his face could make them understand.

Greater Love

Red lips are not so red
    As the stained stones kissed by the English dead.
Kindness of wooed and wooer
Seems shame to their love pure.
O Love, your eyes lose lure
    When I behold eyes blinded in my stead!

Your slender attitude
    Trembles not exquisite like limbs knife-skewed,
Rolling and rolling there
Where God seems not to care;
Till the fierce Love they bear
    Cramps them in death's extreme decrepitude.

Your voice sings not so soft, –
    Though even as wind murmuring through
        raftered loft, –
Your dear voice is not dear,
Gentle, and evening clear,
As theirs whom none now hear

Now earth has stopped their piteous mouths that
    coughed.

Heart, you were never hot,
    Nor large, nor full like hearts made great with shot;
And though your hand be pale,
Paler are all which trail
Your cross through flame and hail:
    Weep, you may weep, for you may touch them not.

Reunion in War

The windmill in his smock of white
  Stared from his little crest,
Like a slow smoke was the moonlight
  As I went like one possessed

Where the glebe path makes shortest way;
  The stammering wicket swung.
I passed amid the crosses grey
  Where opiate yew-boughs hung.

The bleached grass shuddered into sighs,
  The dogs that knew this moon
Far up were harrying sheep, the cries
  Of hunting owls went on.

And I among the dead made haste
  And over flat vault stones
Set in the path unheeding paced
  Nor thought of those chill bones.

Thus to my sweetheart's cottage I,
   Who long had been away,
Turned as the traveller turns adry
   To brooks to moist his clay.

Her cottage stood like a dream, so clear
   And yet so dark; and now
I thought to find my more than dear
   And if she'd kept her vow.

Old house-dog from his barrel came
   Without a voice, and knew
And licked my hand; all seemed the same
   To the moonlight and the dew.

By the white damson then I took
   The tallest osier wand
And thrice upon her casement strook,
   And she, so fair, so fond,

Looked out, and saw in wild delight,
   And tiptoed down to me,
And cried in silent joy that night
   Beside the bullace tree.

O cruel time to take away,
  Or worse to bring agen;
Why slept not I in Flanders clay
  With all the murdered men?

For I had changed, or she had changed,
  Though true loves both had been,
Even while we kissed we stood estranged
  With the ghosts of war between.

We had not met but a moment ere
  War baffled joy, and cried,
'Love's but a madness, a burnt flare;
  The shell's a madman's bride.'

The cottage stood, poor stone and wood,
  Poorer than stone stood I;
Then from her kind arms moved in a mood
  As grey as the cereclothed sky.

The roosts were stirred, each little bird
  Called fearfully out for day;
The church clock with his dead voice whirred
  As if he bade me stay

To trace with foolish fingers all
   The letters on the stones
Where thick beneath the twitch roots crawl
   In dead men's envied bones.

FREDERICK MANNING

Grotesque

These are the damned circles Dante trod,
Terrible in hopelessness,
But even skulls have their humour,
An eyeless and sardonic mockery:
And we,
Sitting with streaming eyes in the acrid smoke,
That murks our foul, damp billet,
Chant bitterly, with raucous voices
As a choir of frogs
In hideous irony, our patriotic songs.

IVOR GURNEY

Butchers and Tombs

After so much battering of fire and steel
It had seemed well to cover them with Cotswold Stone –
And shortly praising their courage and quick skill
Leave them buried, hidden till the slow, inevitable
Change should make them service of France alone.
But the time's hurry, the commonness of the tale,
Made it a thing not fitting ceremonial.
And so the disregarders of blister on heel,
Pack on shoulder, barrage and work at the wires,
One wooden cross had for ensign of honour and life gone –
Save when the Gloucesters turning sudden to tell to one
Some joke, would remember and say – 'That joke is done',
Since he who would understand was so cold he could not
    feel,
And clay binds hard, and sandbags get rotten and crumble.

A Working Party

Three hours ago he blundered up the trench,
Sliding and poising, groping with his boots;
Sometimes he tripped and lurched against the walls
With hands that pawed the sodden bags of chalk.
He couldn't see the man who walked in front;
Only he heard the drum and rattle of feet
Stepping along barred trench boards, often splashing
Wretchedly where the sludge was ankle-deep.

Voices would grunt 'Keep to your right – make way!'
When squeezing past some men from the front-line:
White faces peered, puffing a point of red;
Candles and braziers glinted through the chinks
And curtain-flaps of dug-outs; then the gloom
Swallowed his sense of sight; he stooped and swore
Because a sagging wire had caught his neck.

A flare went up; the shining whiteness spread
And flickered upward, showing nimble rats
And mounds of glimmering sand-bags, bleached with
    rain;

Then the slow silver moment died in dark.
The wind came posting by with chilly gusts
And buffeting at corners, piping thin.
And dreary through the crannies; rifle-shots
Would split and crack and sing along the night,
And shells came calmly through the drizzling air
To burst with hollow bang below the hill.
Three hours ago he stumbled up the trench;
Now he will never walk that road again:
He must be carried back, a jolting lump
Beyond all need of tenderness and care.

He was a young man with a meagre wife
And two small children in a Midland town;
He showed their photographs to all his mates,
And they considered him a decent chap
Who did his work and hadn't much to say,
And always laughed at other people's jokes
Because he hadn't any of his own.

That night when he was busy at his job
Of piling bags along the parapet,
He thought how slow time went, stamping his feet
And blowing on his fingers, pinched with cold.
He thought of getting back by half-past twelve,

And tot of rum to send him warm to sleep
In draughty dug-out frowsty with the fumes
Of coke, and full of snoring weary men.

He pushed another bag along the top,
Craning his body outward; then a flare
Gave one white glimpse of No Man's Land and wire;
And as he dropped his head the instant split
His startled life with lead, and all went out.

WILFRED OWEN
Futility

Move him into the sun –
Gently its touch awoke him once,
At home, whispering of fields unsown.
Always it woke him, even in France,
Until this morning and this snow.
If anything might rouse him now
The kind old sun will know.

Think how it wakes the seeds –
Woke, once, the clays of a cold star.
Are limbs so dear-achieved, are sides
Full-nerved, – still warm, – too hard to stir?
Was it for this the clay grew tall?
– O what made fatuous sunbeams toil
To break earth's sleep at all?

ROBERT GRAVES
Recalling War

Enance and exit wounds are silvered clean,
The track aches only when the rain reminds.
The one-legged man forgets his leg of wood,
The one-armed man his jointed wooden arm.
The blinded man sees with his ears and hands
As much or more than once with both his eyes.
Their war was fought these twenty years ago
And now assumes the nature-look of time,
As when the morning traveller turns and views
His wild night-stumbling carved into a hill.

What, then, was war? No mere discord of flags
But an infection of the common sky
That sagged ominously upon the earth
Even when the season was the airiest May.
Down pressed the sky, and we, oppressed, thrust
    out
Boastful tongue, clenched fist and valiant yard.
Natural infirmities were out of mode,
For Death was young again: patron alone
Of healthy dying, premature fate-spasm.

Fear made fine bed-fellows. Sick with delight
At life's discovered transitoriness,
Our youth became all-flesh and waived the mind.
Never was such antiqueness of romance,
Such tasty honey oozing from the heart.
And old importances came swimming back –
Wine, meat, log-fires, a roof over the head,
A weapon at the thigh, surgeons at call.
Even there was a use again for God –
A word of rage in lack of meat, wine, fire,
In ache of wounds beyond all surgeoning.

War was return of earth to ugly earth,
War was foundering of sublimities,
Extinction of each happy art and faith
By which the world had still kept head in air.
Protesting logic or protesting love,
Until the unendurable moment struck –
The inward scream, the duty to run mad.

And we recall the merry ways of guns –
Nibbling the walls of factory and church
Like a child, piecrust; felling groves of trees
Like a child, dandelions with a switch!

Machine-guns rattle toy-like from a hill,
Down in a row the brave tin-soldiers fall:
A sight to be recalled in elder days
When learnedly the future we devote
To yet more boastful visions of despair.

Trench Raid near Hooge

At an hour before the rosy-fingered
    Morning should come
To wonder again what meant these sties,
These wailing shots, these glaring eyes,
    These moping mum,

Through the black reached strange long rosy
      fingers
    All at one aim
Protending, and bending: down they swept,
Successions of similars after leapt
    And bore red flame

To one small ground of the eastern distance,
    And thunderous touched.
East then and west false dawns fan-flashed
And shut, and gaped; false thunders clashed.
    Who stood and watched

Caught piercing horror from the desperate pit
         Which with ten men
Was centre of this. The blood burnt, feeling
The fierce truth there and the last appealing,
         'Us? Us? Again?'

Nor rosy dawn at last appearing
         Through the icy shade
Might mark without trembling the new deforming
Of earth that had seemed past further storming.
         Her fingers played,

One thought, with something of human pity
         On six or seven
Whose looks were hard to understand,
But that they ceased to care what hand
         Lit earth and heaven.

Disabled

He sat in a wheeled chair, waiting for dark,
And shivered in his ghastly suit of grey,
Legless, sewn short at elbow. Through the park
Voices of boys rang saddening like a hymn,
Voices of play and pleasure after day,
Till gathering sleep had mothered them from him.

About this time Town used to swing so gay
When glow-lamps budded in the light-blue trees
And girls glanced lovelier as the air grew dim,
– In the old times, before he threw away his knees.
Now he will never feel again how slim
Girls' waists are, or how warm their subtle hands,
All of them touch him like some queer disease.

There was an artist silly for his face,
For it was younger than his youth, last year.
Now he is old; his back will never brace;
He's lost his colour very far from here,
Poured it down shell-holes till the veins ran dry,
And half his lifetime lapsed in the hot race,

And leap of purple spurted from his thigh.
One time he liked a bloodsmear down his leg,
After the matches carried shoulder-high.
It was after football, when he'd drunk a peg,
He thought he'd better join. He wonders why . . .
Someone had said he'd look a god in kilts.

That's why; and maybe, too, to please his Meg,
Aye, that was it, to please the giddy jilts,
He asked to join. He didn't have to beg;
Smiling they wrote his lie; aged nineteen years.
Germans he scarcely thought of; and no fears
Of Fear came yet. He thought of jewelled hilts
For daggers in plaid socks; of smart salutes;
And care of arms; and leave; and pay arrears;
Esprit de corps; and hints for young recruits.
And soon, he was drafted out with drums and cheers.

Some cheered him home, but not as crowds cheer
    Goal.
Only a solemn man who brought him fruits
Thanked him; and then inquired about his soul.
Now, he will spend a few sick years in Institutes,
And do what things the rules consider wise,
And take whatever pity they may dole.

Tonight he noticed how the women's eyes
Passed from him to the strong men that were whole.
How cold and late it is! Why don't they come
And put him into bed? Why don't they come?

EDWARD THOMAS
The Cherry Trees

The cherry trees bend over and are shedding,
On the old road where all that passed are dead,
Their petals, strewing the grass as for a wedding
This early May morn when there is none to wed.

EDMUND BLUNDEN
Report on Experience

I have been young, and now am not too old;
And I have seen the righteous forsaken,
His health, his honour and his quality taken.
    This is not what we were formerly told.

I have seen a green country, useful to the race,
Knocked silly with guns and mines, its villages
        vanished,
Even the last rat and last kestrel banished –
    God bless us all, this was peculiar grace.

I knew Seraphina; Nature gave her hue,
Glance, sympathy, note, like one from Eden.
I saw her smile warp, heard her lyric deaden;
    She turned to harlotry; – this I took to be new.

Say what you will, our God sees how they run.
These disillusions are His curious proving
That He loves humanity and will go on loving;
    Over there are faith, life, virtue in the sun.

MARGARET POSTGATE COLE
The Veteran

We came upon him sitting in the sun,
    Blinded by war, and left. And past the fence
There came young soldiers from the Hand and
        Flower,
    Asking advice of his experience.

And he said this, and that, and told them tales,
    And all the nightmares of each empty head
Blew into air; then, hearing us beside,
    'Poor chaps, how'd they know what it's like?'
        he said.

And we stood there, and watched him as he sat,
    Turning his sockets where they went away,
Until it came to one of us to ask
    'And you're – how old?'
            'Nineteen, the third of May.'

WILFRED OWEN
The Show

My soul looked down from a vague height with
 Death,
As unremembering how I rose or why,
And saw a sad land, weak with sweats of dearth,
Gray, cratered like the moon with hollow woe,
And fitted with great pocks and scabs of plaques.

Across its beard, that horror of harsh wire,
There moved thin caterpillars, slowly uncoiled.
It seemed they pushed themselves to be as plugs
Of ditches, where they writhed and shrivelled, killed.

By them had slimy paths been trailed and scraped
Round myriad warts that might be little hills.

From gloom's last dregs these long-strung creatures
 crept,
And vanished out of dawn down hidden holes.

(And smell came up from those foul openings
As out of mouths, or deep wounds deepening.)

On dithering feet upgathered, more and more,
Brown strings towards strings of gray, with bristling
    spines,
All migrants from green fields, intent on mire.

Those that were gray, of more abundant spawns,
Ramped on the rest and ate them and were eaten.

I saw their bitten backs curve, loop, and straighten,
I watched those agonies curl, lift, and flatten.

Whereat, in terror what that sight might mean,
I reeled and shivered earthward like a feather.

And Death fell with me, like a deepening moan.

And He, picking a manner of worm, which half had
    hid
Its bruises in the earth, but crawled no further,
Showed me its feet, the feet of many men,
And the fresh-severed head of it, my head.

The Redeemer

Darkness: the rain sluiced down; the mire was
    deep;
It was past twelve on a mid-winter night,
When peaceful folk in beds lay snug asleep;
There, with much work to do before the light,
We lugged our clay-sucked boots as best we might
Along the trench; sometimes a bullet sang,
And droning shells burst with a hollow bang;
We were soaked, chilled and wretched, every one;
Darkness; the distant wink of a huge gun.

I turned in the black ditch, loathing the storm;
A rocket fizzed and burned with blanching flare,
And lit the face of what had been a form
Floundering in mirk. He stood before me there;
I say that He was Christ; stiff in the glare,
And leaning forward from His burdening task,
Both arms supporting it; His eyes on mine
Stared from the woeful head that seemed a mask
Of mortal pain in Hell's unholy shine.

No thorny crown, only a woollen cap
He wore – an English soldier, white and strong,
Who loved his time like any simple chap,
Good days of work and sport and homely song;
Now he has learned that nights are very long,
And dawn a watching of the windowed sky.
But to the end, unjudging, he'll endure
Horror and pain, not uncontent to die
That Lancaster on Lune may stand secure.

He faced me, reeling in his weariness,
Shouldering his load of planks, so hard to bear.
I say that He was Christ, who wrought to bless
All groping things with freedom bright as air,
And with His mercy washed and made them fair.
Then the flame sank, and all grew black as pitch,
While we began to struggle along the ditch;
And someone flung his burden in the muck,
Mumbling: 'O Christ Almighty, now I'm stuck!'

Strange Service

Little did I dream, England, that you bore me
Under the Cotswold hills beside the water meadows,
To do you dreadful service, here, beyond your borders
And your enfolding seas.

I was a dreamer ever, and bound to your dear service,
Meditating deep, I thought on your secret beauty,
As through a child's face one may see the clear spirit
Miraculously shining.

Your hills not only hills, but friends of mine and kindly,
Your tiny knolls and orchards hidden beside the river
Muddy and strongly-flowing, with shy and tiny
    streamlets
Safe in its bosom.

Now these are memories only, and your skies and rushy
    sky-pools
Fragile mirrors easily broken by moving airs . . .
In my deep heart for ever goes on your daily being,
And uses consecrate.

Think on me too, O Mother, who wrest my soul to
    serve you
In strange and fearful ways beyond your encircling
    waters;
None but you can know my heart, its tears and sacrifice;
None, but you, repay.

Third Ypres

Triumph! How strange, how strong had triumph
    come
On weary hate of foul and endless war
When from its grey gravecloths awoke anew
The summer day. Among the tumbled wreck
Of fascined lines and mounds the light was peering,
Half-smiling upon us, and our newfound pride;
The terror of the waiting night outlived,
The time too crowded for the heart to count
All the sharp cost in friends killed on the assault.
No hook of all the octopus had held us,
Here stood we trampling down the ancient tyrant.
So shouting dug we among the monstrous pits.
Amazing quiet fell upon the waste,
Quiet intolerable to those who felt
The hurrying batteries beyond the masking hills
For their new parley setting themselves in array
In crafty forms unmapped.

                  No, these smiled Faith,
Are dumb for the reason of their overthrow.
They move not back, they lie among the crews

Twisted and choked, they'll never speak again.
Only the copse where once might stand a shrine
Still clacked and suddenly hissed its bullets by.
The War would end, the Line was on the move,
And at a bound the impassable was passed.
We lay and waited with extravagant joy.

Now dulls the day and chills; comes there no word
From those who swept through our new lines to
    flood
The lines beyond? but little comes, and so
Sure as a runner time himself's accosted.
And the slow moments shake their heavy heads,
And croak, 'They're done, they'll none of them get
    through.
They're done, they've all died on the entanglements,
The wire stood up like an unplashed hedge and
    thorned
With giant spikes – and there they've paid the bill.'
Then comes the black assurance, then the sky's
Mute misery lapses into trickling rain,
That wreathes and swims and soon shuts in our
    world,
And those distorted guns, that lay past use,
Why – miracles not over! – all a-firing!

The rain's no cloak from their sharp eyes. And you,
Poor signaller, you I passed by this emplacement,
You whom I warned, poor daredevil, waving your
    flags,
Among this screeching I pass you again and shudder
At the lean green flies upon the red flesh madding.
Runner, stand by a second. Your message. – He's
    gone,
Falls on a knee, and his right hand uplifted
Claws his last message from his ghostly enemy,
Turns stone-like. Well I liked him, that young
    runner,
But there's no time for that. O now for the word
To order us flash from these drowning roaring traps
And even hurl upon that snarling wire?
Why are our guns so impotent?
                        The grey rain,
Steady as the sand in an hourglass on this day,
Where through the window the red lilac looks,
And all's so still, the chair's odd click is noise –
The rain is all heaven's answer, and with hearts
Past reckoning we are carried into night
And even sleep is nodding here and there.
The second night steals through the shrouding rain.
We in our numb thought crouching long have lost

The mockery triumph, and in every runner
Have urged the mind's eye see the triumph to come
The sweet relief, the straggling out of hell
Into whatever burrows may be given
For life's recall. Then the fierce destiny speaks.
This was the calm, we shall look back for this.
The hour is come; come, move to the relief!
Dizzy we pass the mule-strewn track where once
The ploughman whistled as he loosed his team;
And where he turned home-hungry on the road,
The leaning pollard marks us hungrier turning.
We crawl to save the remnant who have torn
Back from the tentacled wire, those whom no shell
Has charred into black carcasses – Relief!
They grate their teeth until we take their room,
And through the churn of moonless night and mud
And flaming burst and sour gas we are huddled
Into the ditches where they bawl sense awake,
And in a frenzy that none could reason calm
(Whimpering some, and calling on the dead),
They turn away: as in a dream they find
Strength in their feet to bear back that strange whim
Their body.

    At the noon of the dreadful day
Our trench and death's is on a sudden stormed

With huge and shattering salvoes, the clay dances
In founts of clods around the concrete sties,
Where still the brain devises some last armour
To live out the poor limbs.
                      This wrath's oncoming
Found four of us together in a pillbox,
Skirting the abyss of madness with light phrases,
White and blinking, in false smiles grimacing.
The demon grins to see the game, a moment
Passes, and – still the drum-tap dongs my brain
To a whirring void – through the great breach above
    me
The light comes in with icy shock and the rain
Horribly drips. Doctor, talk, talk! if dead
Or stunned I know not; the stinking powdered
    concrete,
The lyddite turns me sick – my hair's all full
Of this smashed concrete. O, I'll drag you, friends,
Out of the sepulchre into the light of day,
For this is day, the pure and sacred day.
And while I squeak and gibber over you,
Look, from the wreck a score of field-mice nimble,
And tame and curious look about them; (these
Calmed me, on these depended my salvation).
There comes my sergeant, and by all the powers

The wire is holding to the right battalion,
And I can speak – but I myself first spoken
Hear a known voice now measured even to madness
Call me by name.
                              'For God's sake send and help us,
Here in a gunpit, all headquarters done for,
Forty or more, the nine-inch came right through,
All splashed with arms and legs, and I myself
The only one not killed nor even wounded.
You'll send – God bless you!' The more monstrous
      fate
Shadows our own, the mind swoons doubly
      burdened,
Taught how for miles our anguish groans and bleeds,
A whole sweet countryside amuck with murder;
Each moment puffed into a year with death
Still wept the rain, roared guns,
Still swooped into the swamps of flesh and blood,
All to the drabness of uncreation sunk,
And all thought dwindled to a moan, Relieve!
But who with what command can now relieve
The dead men from that chaos, or my soul?

EDWARD THOMAS
The Owl

Downhill I came, hungry, and yet not starved;
Cold, yet had heat within me that was proof
Against the North wind; tired, yet so that rest
Had seemed the sweetest thing under a roof.

Then at the inn I had food, fire, and rest,
Knowing how hungry, cold, and tired was I.
All of the night was quite barred out except
An owl's cry, a most melancholy cry

Shaken out long and clear upon the hill,
No merry note, nor cause of merriment,
But one telling me plain what I escaped
And others could not, that night, as in I went.

And salted was my food, and my repose,
Salted and sobered, too, by the bird's voice
Speaking for all who lay under the stars,
Soldiers and poor, unable to rejoice.

CHARLES HAMILTON SORLEY

Two Sonnets

I

Saints have adored the lofty soul of you.
Poets have whitened at your high renown.
We stand among the many millions who
Do hourly wait to pass your pathway down.
You, so familiar, once were strange: we tried
To live as of your presence unaware.
But now in every road on every side
We see your straight and steadfast signpost
    there.

I think it like that signpost in my land,
Hoary and tall, which pointed me to go
Upward, into the hills, on the right hand,
Where the mists swim and the winds shriek and
    blow,
A homeless land and friendless, but a land
I did not know and that I wished to know.

Such, such is Death: no triumph: no defeat:
Only an empty pail, a slate rubbed clean,
A merciful putting away of what has been.

And this we know: Death is not Life effete,
Life crushed, the broken pail. We who have seen
So marvellous things know well the end not yet.

Victor and vanquished are a-one in death:
Coward and brave: friend, foe. Ghosts do not say
'Come, what was your record when you drew
    breath?'
But a big blot has hid each yesterday
So poor, so manifestly incomplete.
And your bright Promise, withered long and
    sped,
Is touched, stirs, rises, opens and grows sweet
And blossoms and is you, when you are dead.

Banishment

I am banished from the patient men who fight
They smote my heart to pity, built my pride.
Shoulder to aching shoulder, side by side,
They trudged away from life's broad wealds of light.
Their wrongs were mine; and ever in my sight
They went arrayed in honour. But they died, –
Not one by one: and mutinous I cried
To those who sent them out into the night.

The darkness tells how vainly I have striven
To free them from the pit where they must dwell
In outcast gloom convulsed and jagged and riven
By grappling guns. Love drove me to rebel.
Love drives me back to grope with them through hell;
And in their tortured eyes I stand forgiven.

WILFRED OWEN
Arms and the Boy

Let the boy try along this bayonet-blade
How cold steel is, and keen with hunger of blood;
Blue with all malice, like a madman's flash;
And thinly drawn with famishing for flesh.

Lend him to stroke these blind, blunt bullet-heads
Which long to muzzle in the hearts of lads.
Or give him cartridges of fine zinc teeth,
Sharp with the sharpness of grief and death.

For his teeth seem for laughing round an apple.
There lurk no claws behind his fingers supple;
And God will grow no talons at his heels,
Nor antlers through the thickness of his curls.

EDMUND BLUNDEN
Preparations for Victory

My soul, dread not the pestilence that hags
The valley; flinch not you, my body young,
At these great shouting smokes and snarling jags
Of fiery iron; as yet may not be flung
The dice that claims you. Manly move among
These ruins, and what you must do, do well;
Look, here are gardens, there mossed boughs are hung
With apples whose bright cheeks none might excel,
And there's a house as yet unshattered by a shell.

'I'll do my best,' the soul makes sad reply,
'And I will mark the yet unmurdered tree,
The tokens of dear homes that court the eye,
And yet I see them not as I would see.
Hovering between, a ghostly enemy,
Sickens the light, and poisoned, withered, wan,
The least defiled turns desperate to me.'
The body, poor unpitied Caliban,
Parches and sweats and grunts to win the name of Man.

Days or eternities like swelling waves
Surge on, and still we drudge in this dark maze;
The bombs and coils and cans by strings of slaves
Are borne to serve the coming day of days;
Pale sleep in slimy cellars scarce allays
With its brief blank the burden. Look, we lose;
The sky is gone, the lightless, drenching haze
Of rainstorm chills the bone; earth, air are foes,
The black fiend leaps brick-red as life's last picture goes.

Pain

Pain, pain continual; pain unending;
Hard even to the roughest, but to those
Hungry for beauty . . . Not the wisest knows,
Nor most pitiful-hearted, what the wending
Of one hour's way meant. Grey monotony lending
Weight to the grey skies, grey mud where goes
An army of grey bedrenched scarecrows in rows
Careless at last of cruellest Fate-sending.
Seeing the pitiful eyes of men foredone,
Or horses shot, too tired merely to stir,
Dying in shell-holes both, slain by the mud.
Men broken, shrieking even to hear a gun.
Till pain grinds down, or lethargy numbs her,
The amazed heart cries angrily out on God.

Repression of War Experience

Now light the candles; one; two; there's a moth;
What silly beggars they are to blunder in
And scorch their wings with glory, liquid flame –
No, no, not that, – it's bad to think of war,
When thoughts you've gagged all day come back to
    scare you;
And it's been proved that soldiers don't go mad
Unless they lose control of ugly thoughts
That drive them out to jabber among the trees.

Now light your pipe; look, what a steady hand.
Draw a deep breath; stop thinking; count fifteen,
And you're as right as rain . . .
                Why won't it rain? . . .
I wish there'd be a thunder-storm to-night,
With bucketsful of water to sluice the dark,
And make the roses hang their dripping heads.
Books; what a jolly company they are,
Standing so quiet and patient on their shelves,
Dressed in dim brown, and black, and white, and green,
And every kind of colour. Which will you read?

Come on; O *do* read something; they're so wise.
I tell you all the wisdom of the world
Is waiting for you on those shelves; and yet
You sit and gnaw your nails, and let your pipe out,
And listen to the silence: on the ceiling
There's one big, dizzy moth that bumps and flutters;
And in the breathless air outside the house
The garden waits for something that delays.
There must be crowds of ghosts among the trees, –
Not people killed in battle, – they're in France, –
But horrible shapes in shrouds – old men who died
Slow, natural deaths, – old men with ugly souls,
Who wore their bodies out with nasty sins.

You're quiet and peaceful, summering safe at home;
You'd never think there was a bloody war on! . . .
O yes, you would . . . why, you can hear the guns.
Hark! Thud, thud, thud, – quite soft . . . they never
        cease –
Those whispering guns – O Christ, I want to go out
And screech at them to stop – I'm going crazy;
I'm going stark, staring mad because of the guns.

The Send-off

Down the close, darkening lanes they sang their way
To the siding-shed,
And lined the train with faces grimly gay.

Their breasts were stuck all white with wreath and
    spray
As men's are, dead.

Dull porters watched them, and a casual tramp
Stood staring hard,
Sorry to miss them from the upland camp.
Then, unmoved, signals nodded, and a lamp
Winked to the guard.

So secretly, like wrongs hushed-up, they went.
They were not ours:
We never heard to which front these were sent.

Nor there if they yet mock what women meant
Who gave them flowers.

Shall they return to beatings of great bells
In wild trainloads?
A few, a few, too few for drums and yells,
May creep back, silent, to still village wells
Up half-known roads.

SIEGFRIED SASSOON
Glory of Women

You love us when we're heroes, home on leave,
Or wounded in a mentionable place.
You worship decorations; you believe
That chivalry redeems the war's disgrace.
You make us shells. You listen with delight,
By tales of dirt and danger fondly thrilled.
You crown our distant ardours while we fight,
And mourn our laurelled memories when we're
          killed.
You can't believe that British troops 'retire'
When hell's last horror breaks them, and they run,
Trampling the terrible corpses – blind with blood.
    O German mother dreaming by the fire,
    While you are knitting socks to send your son
    His face is trodden deeper in the mud.

THOMAS HARDY
Channel Firing

That night your great guns, unawares,
Shook all our coffins as we lay,
And broke the chancel window-squares,
We thought it was the Judgment-day.

And sat upright. While drearisome
Arose the howl of wakened hounds:
The mouse let fall the altar-crumb,
The worms drew back into the mounds,

The glebe cow drooled. Till God called, 'No;
It's gunnery practice out at sea
Just as before you went below;
The world is as it used to be:

'All nations striving strong to make
Red war yet redder. Mad as hatters
They do no more for Christés sake
Than you who are helpless in such matters.

'That this is not the judgment-hour
For some of them's a blessed thing,
For if it were they'd have to scour
Hell's floor for so much threatening . . .

'Ha, ha. It will be warmer when
I blow the trumpet (if indeed
I ever do; for you are men,
And rest eternal sorely need).'

So down we lay again. 'I wonder,
Will the world ever saner be,'
Said one, 'than when He sent us under
In our indifferent century!'

And many a skeleton shook his head.
'Instead of preaching forty year,'
My neighbour Parson Thirdly said,
'I wish I had stuck to pipes and beer.'

Again the guns disturbed the hour,
Roaring their readiness to avenge,
As far inland as Stourton Tower,
And Camelot, and starlit Stonehenge.

The Sentry

We'd found an old Boche dug-out, and he knew,
And gave us hell, for shell on frantic shell
Hammered on top, but never quite burst through.
Rain, guttering down in waterfalls of slime
Kept slush waist high, that rising hour by hour,
Choked up the steps too thick with clay to climb.
What murk of air remained stank old, and sour
With fumes of whizz-bangs, and the smell of men
Who'd lived there years, and left their curse in the den,
If not their corpses . . .

                    There we herded from the blast
Of whizz-bangs, but one found our door at last.
Buffeting eyes and breath, snuffing the candles.
And thud! flump! thud! down the steep steps came
    thumping
And splashing in the flood, deluging muck –
The sentry's body; then his rifle, handles
Of old Boche bombs, and mud in ruck on ruck.
We dredged him up, for killed, until he whined
'O sir, my eyes – I'm blind – I'm blind, I'm blind!'
Coaxing, I held a flame against his lids

And said if he could see the least blurred light
He was not blind; in time he'd get all right.
'I can't,' he sobbed. Eyeballs, huge-bulged like squids
Watch my dreams still; but I forgot him there
In posting next for duty, and sending a scout
To beg a stretcher somewhere, and floundering about
To other posts under the shrieking air.

Those other wretches, how they bled and spewed,
And one who would have drowned himself for good, –
I try not to remember these things now.
Let dread hark back for one word only: how
Half-listening to that sentry's moans and jumps,
And the wild chattering of his broken teeth,
Renewed most horribly whenever crumps
Pummelled the roof and slogged the air beneath –
Through the dense din, I say, we heard him shout
'I see your lights!' But ours had long died out.

IVOR GURNEY

De Profundis

If only this fear would leave me I could dream of Crickley
  Hill
    And a hundred thousand thoughts of home would visit
      my heart in sleep;
But here the peace is shattered all day by the devil's will,
    And the guns bark night-long to spoil the velvet silence
      deep.

O who could think that once we drank in quiet inns and
      cool
    And saw brown oxen trooping the dry sands to slake
Their thirst at the river flowing, or plunged in a silver pool
    To shake the sleepy drowse off before well awake?

We are stale here, we are covered body and soul and mind
    With mire of the trenches, close clinging and foul.
We have left our old inheritance, our Paradise behind,
    And clarity is lost to us and cleanness of soul.

O blow here, you dusk-airs and breaths of half-light,
    And comfort despairs of your darlings that long
Night and day for sound of your bells, or a sight
    Of your tree-bordered lanes, land of blossom and song.

Autumn will be here soon, but the road of coloured leaves
    Is not for us, the up and down highway where go
Earth's pilgrims to wonder where Malvern upheaves
    That blue-emerald splendour under great clouds of snow.

Some day we'll fill in trenches, level the land and turn
    Once more joyful faces to the country where trees
Bear thickly for good drink, where strong sunsets burn
    Huge bonfires of glory – O God, send us peace!

Hard it is for men of moors or fens to endure
    Exile and hardship, or the northland grey-drear;
But we of the rich plain of sweet airs and pure,
    Oh! Death would take so much from us, how should we
        not fear?

SIEGFRIED SASSOON
Suicide in the Trenches

I knew a simple soldier boy
Who grinned at life in empty joy,
Slept soundly through the lonesome dark,
And whistled early with the lark.

In winter trenches, cowed and glum,
With crumps and lice and lack of rum,
He put a bullet through his brain.
No one spoke of him again.

You smug-faced crowds with kindling eye
Who cheer when soldier lads march by,
Sneak home and pray you'll never know
The hell where youth and laughter go.

Strange Meeting

It seemed that out of the battle I escaped
Down some profound dull tunnel, long since scooped
Through granites which Titanic wars had groined.
Yet also there encumbered sleepers groaned,
Too fast in thought or death to be bestirred.
Then, as I probed them, one sprang up, and stared
With piteous recognition in fixed eyes,
Lifting distressful hands as if to bless.
And by his smile, I knew that sullen hall;
With a thousand fears that vision's face was grained;
Yet no blood reached there from the upper ground,
And no guns thumped, or down the flues made moan.
'Strange, friend,' I said, 'Here is no cause to mourn.'
'None,' said the other, 'Save the undone years
The hopelessness. Whatever hope is yours,
Was my life also; I went hunting wild
After the wildest beauty in the world,
Which lies not calm in eyes, or braided hair,
But mocks the steady running of the hour,
And if it grieves, grieves richlier than here.
For by my glee might many men have laughed,

And of my weeping something has been left,
Which must die now. I mean the truth untold,
The pity of war, the pity war distilled.
Now men will go content with what we spoiled.
Or, discontent, boil bloody, and be spilled.
They will be swift with swiftness of the tigress,
None will break ranks, though nations trek from
   progress.
Courage was mine, and I had mystery;
Wisdom was mine, and I had mastery;
To miss the march of this retreating world
Into vain citadels that are not walled.
Then, when much blood had clogged their
   chariot-wheels
I would go up and wash them from sweet wells,
Even with truths that lie too deep for taint.
I would have poured my spirit without stint
But not through wounds; not on the cess of war.
Foreheads of men have bled where no wounds were.
I am the enemy you killed, my friend.
I knew you in this dark; for so you frowned
Yesterday through me as you jabbed and killed.
I parried; but my hands were loath and cold.
Let us sleep now . . .'

Lament

The young men of the world
Are condemned to death.
They have been called up to die
For the crime of their fathers.

The young men of the world,
The growing, the ripening fruit,
Have been torn from their branches,
While the memory of the blossom
Is sweet in women's hearts;
They have been cast for a cruel purpose
Into the mashing-press and furnace.

The young men of the world
Look into each other's eyes,
And read there the same words:
Not yet! Not yet!
But soon perhaps, and perhaps certain.

The young men of the world
No longer possess the road:
The road possesses them.
They no longer inherit the earth:
The earth inherits them.
They are no longer the masters of fire:
Fire is their master;
They serve him, he destroys them.
They no longer rule the waters:
The genius of the seas
Has invented a new monster,
And they fly from its teeth.
They no longer breathe freely:
The genius of the air
Has contrived a new terror
That rends them into pieces.

The young men of the world
Are encompassed with death
He is all about them
In a circle of fire and bayonets.

Weep, weep, o women,
and old men break your hearts.

WILFRED OWEN
Exposure

I

Our brains ache, in the merciless iced east winds that
    knife us . . .
Wearied we keep awake because the night is silent . . .
Low drooping flares confuse our memory of the salient . . .
Worried by silence, sentries whisper, curious, nervous,
        But nothing happens.

Watching, we hear the mad gusts tugging on the wire.
Like twitching agonies of men among its brambles.
Northward incessantly, the flickering gunnery rumbles,
Far off, like a dull rumour of some other war.
       What are we doing here?

The poignant misery of dawn begins to grow . . .
We only know war lasts, rain soaks, and clouds sag stormy.
Dawn massing in the east her melancholy army
Attacks once more in ranks on shivering ranks of gray.
       But nothing happens.

Sudden successive flights of bullets streak the silence.
Less deadly than the air that shudders black with snow,
With sidelong flowing flakes that flock, pause and renew,
We watch them wandering up and down the wind's
  nonchalance,
   But nothing happens.

II

Pale flakes with lingering stealth come feeling for our
  faces –
We cringe in holes, back on forgotten dreams, and stare,
  snow-dazed.
Deep into grassier ditches. So we drowse, sun-dozed,
Littered with blossoms trickling where the blackbird
  fusses.
   Is it that we are dying?

Slowly our ghosts drag home: glimpsing the sunk fires
  glozed
With crusted dark-red jewels; crickets jingle there;
For hours the innocent mice rejoice: the house is theirs;
Shutters and doors all closed: on us the doors are closed –
   We turn back to our dying.

Since we believe not otherwise can kind fires burn;
Now ever suns smile true on child, or field, or fruit.
For God's invincible spring our love is made afraid;
Therefore, not loath, we lie out here; therefore
    were born,
        For love of God seems dying.

Tonight, His frost will fasten on this mud and us,
Shrivelling many hands and puckering foreheads crisp.
The burying-party, picks and shovels in their
    shaking grasp,
Pause over half-known faces. All their eyes are ice,
        But nothing happens.

Counter-Attack

We'd gained our first objective hours before
While dawn broke like a face with blinking eyes,
Pallid, unshaved and thirsty, blind with smoke.
Things seemed all right at first. We held their line,
With bombers posted, Lewis guns well placed,
And clink of shovels deepening the shallow trench.
   The place was rotten with dead; green clumsy legs
   High-booted, sprawled and grovelled along the saps
   And trunks, face downward, in the sucking mud,
   Wallowed like trodden sand-bags loosely filled;
   And naked sodden buttocks, mats of hair,
   Bulged, clotted heads slept in the plastering slime,
   And then the rain began, – the jolly old rain!

A yawning soldier knelt against the bank,
Staring across the morning blear with fog;
He wondered when the Allemands would get busy;
And then, of course, they started with five-nines
Traversing, sure as fate, and never a dud.
Mute in the clamour of shells he watched them burst
Spouting dark earth and wire with gusts from hell,

While posturing giants dissolved in drifts of smoke.
He crouched and flinched, dizzy with galloping fear,
Sick for escape, – loathing the strangled horror
And butchered, frantic gestures of the dead.

An officer came blundering down the trench:
'Stand-to and man the fire-step!' On he went . . .
Gasping and bawling, 'Fire-step . . . counter-attack!'

   Then the haze lifted. Bombing on the right
   Down the old sap: machine-guns on the left;
   And stumbling figures looming out in front.
   'O Christ, they're coming at us!' Bullets spat,
And he remembered his rifle . . . rapid fire . . .
And started blazing wildly . . . then a bang
Crumpled and spun him sideways, knocked him out
To grunt and wriggle: none heeded him; he choked
And fought the flapping veils of smothering gloom,
Lost in a blurred confusion of yells and groans . . .
Down, and down, and down, he sank and drowned,
Bleeding to death. The counter-attack had failed.

IVOR GURNEY

Photographs
(To Two Scots Lads)

Lying in dug-outs, joking idly, wearily;
  Watching the candle guttering in the draught;
Hearing the great shells go high over us, eerily
  Singing; how often have I turned over, and laughed

With pity and pride, photographs of all colours,
  All sizes, subjects: khaki brothers in France;
Or mothers' faces worn with countless dolours;
  Or girls whose eyes were challenging and must dance,

Though in a picture only, a common cheap
  Ill-taken card; and children – frozen, some
(Babies) waiting on Dicky-bird to peep
  Out of the handkerchief that is his home

(But he's so shy!). And some with bright looks, calling
  Delight across the miles of land and sea,
That not the dread of barrage suddenly falling
  Could quite blot out – not mud nor lethargy.

Smiles and triumphant careless laughter. O
    The pain of them, wide Earth's most sacred things!
Lying in dug-outs, hearing the great shells slow.
    Sailing mile-high, the heart mounts higher and sings.

But once – O why did he keep that bitter token
    Of a dead Love? – that boy, who, suddenly moved,
Showed me, his eyes wet, his low talk broken,
    A girl who better had not been beloved.

Spring Offensive

Halted against the shade of a last hill,
They fed, and, lying easy, were at ease
And, finding comfortable chests and knees
Carelessly slept. But many there stood still
To face the stark, blank sky beyond the ridge,
Knowing their feet had come to the end of the world.

Marvelling they stood, and watched the long grass swirled
By the May breeze, murmurous with wasp and midge,
For though the summer oozed into their veins
Like the injected drug for their bones' pains,
Sharp on their souls hung the imminent line of grass,
Fearfully flashed the sky's mysterious glass.

Hour after hour they ponder the warm field –
And the far valley behind, where the buttercups
Had blessed with gold their slow boots coming up.
Where even the little brambles would not yield,
But clutched and clung to them like sorrowing hands;
They breathe like trees unstirred.

Till like a cold gust shrilled the little word
At which each body and its soul begird
And tighten them for battle. No alarms
Of bugles, no high flags, no clamorous haste –
Only a lift and flare of eyes that faced
The sun, like a friend with whom their love is done.
O larger shone that smile against the sun, –
Mightier than his whose bounty these have spurned.

So, soon they topped the hill, and raced together
Over an open stretch of herb and heather
Exposed. And instantly the whole sky burned
With fury against them; and soft sudden cups
Opened in thousands for their blood; and the green slopes
Chasmed and steepened sheer to infinite space.

Of them who running on that last high place
Leapt to swift unseen bullets, or went up
On the hot blast and fury of hell's upsurge,
Or plunged and fell away past this world's verge,
Some say God caught them even before they fell.

But what say such as from existence' brink
Ventured but drave too swift to sink.
The few who rushed in the body to enter hell,

And there out-fiending all its fiends and flames
With superhuman inhumanities,
Long-famous glories, immemorial shames –
And crawling slowly back, have by degrees
Regained cool peaceful air in wonder –
Why speak they not of comrades that went under?

ALICE MEYNELL
Summer in England, 1914

On London fell a clearer light;
　　Caressing pencils of the sun
Defined the distances, the white
　　Houses transfigured one by one,
The 'long, unlovely street' impearled.
O what a sky has walked the world!

Most happy year! And out of town
　　The hay was prosperous, and the wheat;
The silken harvest climbed the down:
　　Moon after moon was heavenly-sweet,
Stroking the bread within the sheaves,
Looking 'twixt apples and their leaves.

And while this rose made round her cup,
　　The armies died convulsed. And when
This chaste young silver sun went up
　　Softly, a thousand shattered men,
One wet corruption, heaped the plain,
After a league-long throb of pain.

Flower following tender flower; and birds,
  And berries; and benignant skies
Made thrive the serried flocks and herds. –
  Yonder are men shot through the eyes.
          Love, hide thy face
From man's unpardonable race.

Who said 'No man hath greater love than this,
  To die to serve his friend'?
So these have loved us all unto the end.
  Chide thou no more, O thou unsacrificed!
The soldier dying dies upon a kiss,
  The very kiss of Christ.

Lamentations

I found him in the guard-room at the Base.
From the blind darkness I had heard his crying
And blundered in. With puzzled, patient face
A sergeant watched him; it was no good trying
To stop it; for he howled and beat his chest.
And, all because his brother had gone west,
Raved at the bleeding war; his rampant grief
Moaned, shouted, sobbed, and choked, while he was
     kneeling
Half-naked on the floor. In my belief
Such men have lost all patriotic feeling.

Conscious

His fingers wake, and flutter up the bed.
His eyes come open with a pull of will,
Helped by the yellow may-flowers by his head.
A blind-cord drawls across the window-sill . . .
How smooth the floor of the ward is! what a rug!
And who's that talking, somewhere out of sight?
Why are they laughing? What's inside that jug?
'Nurse! Doctor!' 'Yes; all right, all right.'

But sudden dusk bewilders all the air –
There seems no time to want a drink of water.
Nurse looks so far away. And everywhere
Music and roses burnt through crimson slaughter.
Cold; cold; he's cold; and yet so hot:
And there's no light to see the voices by –
No time to dream, and ask – he knows not what.

IVOR GURNEY

To the Prussians of England

When I remember plain heroic strength
And shining virtue shown by Ypres pools,
Then read the blither written by knaves for fools
In praise of English soldiers lying at length,
Who purely dream what England shall be made
Gloriously new, free of the old stains
By us, who pay the price that must be paid,
Will freeze all winter over Ypres plains.
Our silly dreams of peace you put aside
And brotherhood of man, for you will see
An armed mistress, braggart of the tide,
Her children slaves, under your mastery.
We'll have a word there too, and forge a knife,
Will cut the cancer threatens England's life.

The Hero

'Jack fell as he'd have wished,' the Mother said,
And folded up the letter that she'd read.
'The Colonel writes so nicely.' Something broke
In the tired voice that quavered to a choke.
She half looked up. 'We mothers are so proud
Of our dead soldiers.' Then her face was bowed.

Quietly the Brother Officer went out.
He'd told the poor old dear some gallant lies
That she would nourish all her days, no doubt.
For while he coughed and mumbled, her weak eyes
Had shone with gentle triumph, brimmed with joy,
Because he'd been so brave, her glorious boy.

He thought how 'Jack', cold-footed, useless swine,
Had panicked down the trench that night the mine
Went up at Wicked Corner; how he'd tried
To get sent home, and how, at last, he died,
Blown to small bits. And no one seemed to care
Except that lonely woman with white hair.

The Welcome

He'd scarcely come from leave and London,
Still was carrying a leather case,
When he surprised Headquarters pillbox
And sat down sweating in the filthy place.

He was a tall, lean, pale-looked creature,
With nerves that seldom ceased to wince,
Past war had long preyed on his nature,
And war had doubled in horror since.

There was a lull, the adjutant even
Came to my hole: You cheerful sinner,
If nothing happens till half-past seven,
Come over then, we're going to have dinner.

Back he went with his fierce red head;
We were sourly canvassing his jauntiness, when
Something happened at headquarters pillbox.
'Don't go there,' cried one of my men.

The shell had struck right into the doorway,
The smoke lazily floated away;
There were six men in that concrete doorway,
Now a black muckheap blocked the way.

Inside, one who had scarcely shaken
The air of England out of his lungs
Was alive, and sane; it shall be spoken
While any of those who were there have tongues.

Apologia pro Poemate Meo

I, too, saw God through mud –
> The mud that cracked on cheeks when wretches
> smiled.
> War brought more glory to their eyes than blood,
> And gave their laughs more glee than shakes a child.

Merry it was to laugh there –
> Where death becomes absurd and life absurder.
> For power was on us as we slashed bones bare
> Not to feel sickness or remorse of murder.

I, too, have dropped off fear –
> Behind the barrage, dead as my platoon,
> And sailed my spirit surging, light and clear
> Past the entanglement where hopes lay strewn;

And witnessed exultation –
> Faces that used to curse me, scowl for scowl,
> Shine and lift up with passion of oblation,
> Seraphic for an hour; though they were foul.

I have made fellowships
  Untold of happy lovers in old song.
  For love is not the binding of fair lips
  With the soft silk of eyes that look and long.

By Joy, whose ribbon slips, –
  But wound with war's hard wire whose stakes are
    strong;
  Bound with the bandage of the arm that drips;
  Knit in the welding of the rifle-thong.

I have perceived much beauty
  In the hoarse oaths that kept our courage straight;
  Heard music in the silentness of duty;
  Found peace where shell-storms spouted reddest spate.

Nevertheless, except you share
  With them in hell the sorrowful dark of hell,
  Whose world is but the trembling of a flare,
  And heaven but as the highway for a shell,

You shall not hear their mirth:
  You shall not come to think them well content
  By any jest of mine. These men are worth
  Your tears: You are not worth their merriment.

SIEGFRIED SASSOON
Attack

At dawn the ridge emerges massed and dun
In the wild purple of the glow'ring sun,
Smouldering through spouts of drifting smoke that
    shroud
The menacing scarred slope; and, one by one,
Tanks creep and topple forward to the wire.
The barrage roars and lifts. Then, clumsily bowed
With bombs and guns and shovels and battle-gear,
Men jostle and climb to meet the bristling fire.
Lines of grey, muttering faces, masked with fear,
They leave their trenches, going over the top,
While time ticks blank and busy on their wrists,
And hope, with furtive eyes and grappling fists,
Flounders in mud. O Jesus, make it stop!

Wild with all Regrets
(Another version of 'A Terre')

TO SIEGFRIED SASSOON

My arms have mutinied against me – brutes!
My fingers fidget like ten idle brats,
My back's been stiff for hours, damned hours.
Death never gives his squad a Stand-at-ease.
I can't read. There: It's no use. Take your book.
A short life and a merry one, my buck!
We said we'd hate to grow dead old. But now,
Not to live old seems awful: not to renew
My boyhood with my boys, and teach 'em hitting,
Shooting and hunting, – all the arts of hurting!
– Well, that's what I learnt. That, and making
        money.
Your fifty years in store seem none too many;
But I've five minutes. God! For just two years
To help myself to this good air of yours!
One Spring! Is one too hard to spare? Too long?
Spring air would find its own way to my lung,
And grow me legs as quick as lilac-shoots.

Yes, there's the orderly. He'll change the sheets
When I'm lugged out, oh, couldn't I do that?
Here in this coffin of a bed, I've thought
I'd like to kneel and sweep his floors for ever, –
And ask no nights off when the bustle's over,
For I'd enjoy the dirt; who's prejudiced
Against a grimed hand when his own's quite dust, –
Less live than specks that in the sun-shafts turn?
Dear dust, – in rooms, on roads, on faces' tan!
I'd love to be a sweep's boy, black as Town;
Yes, or a muckman. Must I be his load?
A flea would do. If one chap wasn't bloody,
Or went stone-cold, I'd find another body.

Which I shan't manage now. Unless it's yours.
I shall stay in you, friend, for some few hours.
You'll feel my heavy spirit chill your chest,
And climb your throat on sobs, until it's chased
On sighs, and wiped from off your lips by wind.

I think on your rich breathing, brother, I'll be
    weaned
To do without what blood remained me from my
    wound.

In the Trenches

1

Not that we are weary,
Not that we fear,
Not that we are lonely
Though never alone –
Not these, not these destroy us;
But that each rush and crash
Of mortar and shell,
Each cruel bitter shriek of bullet
That tears the wind like a blade,
Each wound on the breast of earth,
Of Demeter, our Mother,
Wound us also,
Sever and rend the fine fabric
Of the wings of our frail souls,
Scatter into dust the bright wings
Of Psyche!

2

Impotent,
How impotent is all this clamour,
This destruction and contest . . .
Night after night comes the moon
Haughty and perfect;
Night after night the Pleiades sing
And Orion swings his belt across the sky.
Night after night the frost
Crumbles the hard earth.

Soon the spring will drop flowers
And patient creeping stalk and leaf
Along these barren lines
Where the huge rats scuttle
And the hawk shrieks to the carrion crow.

WILFRED OWEN
The End

After the blast of lightning from the east,
The flourish of loud clouds, the Chariot throne,
After the drums of time have rolled and ceased
And from the bronze west long retreat is blown,

Shall Life renew these bodies? Of a truth
All death will he annul, all tears assuage?
Or fill these void veins full again with youth
And wash with an immortal water age?

When I do ask white Age, he saith not so, –
'My head hangs weighed with snow.'
And when I hearken to the Earth she saith
'My fiery heart sinks aching. It is death.
Mine ancient scars shall not be glorified
Nor my titanic tears the seas be dried.'

SIEGFRIED SASSOON
Does it Matter?

Does it matter? – losing your legs? . . .
For people will always be kind,
And you need not show that you mind
When the others come in after hunting
To gobble their muffins and eggs.

Does it matter? – losing your sight? . . .
There's such splendid work for the blind;
And people will always be kind,
As you sit on the terrace remembering
And turning your face to the light.

Do they matter? – those dreams from the pit? . . .
You can drink and forget and be glad,
And people won't say that you're mad;
For they'll know you've fought for your country
And no one will worry a bit.

Lamplight

We planned to shake the world together, you and I
Being young, and very wise;
Now in the light of the green shaded lamp
Almost I see your eyes
Light with the old gay laughter; you and I
Dreamed greatly of an Empire in those days,
Setting our feet upon laborious ways,
And all you asked of fame
Was crossed swords in the Army List,
My Dear, against your name.

We planned a great Empire together, you and I,
Bound only by the sea;
Now in the quiet of a chill Winter's night
Your voice comes hushed to me
Full of forgotten memories: you and I
Dreamed great dreams of our future in those days,
Setting our feet on undiscovered ways,
And all I asked of fame
A scarlet cross on my breast, my Dear,
For the swords by your name.

We shall never shake the world together, you and I,
For you gave your life away;
And I think my heart was broken by the war,
Since on a summer day
You took the road we never spoke of: you and I
Dreamed greatly of an Empire in those days;
You set your feet upon the Western ways
And have no need of fame –
There's scarlet cross on my breast, my Dear,
And a torn cross with your name.